GENERATION
CODE

I'M AN
APP DEVELOPER

Max Wainewright

WAYLAND
www.waylandbooks.co.uk

CONTENTS

 RESPECTING COPYRIGHT

Copyright means the legal ownership of something. You need to think about who owns the images or sound files you are linking to or downloading in your apps. There shouldn't be any major issues unless you try to make an app available to the public. Do check with an adult to make sure.

An alternative is to find a free to use image or sound file: search for an image or sound, then look for the **Settings** button on the website results page. Click **Advanced Search** then look for **Usage Rights**. On this menu choose **Free to use, share or modify**.

INTRODUCTION

In this book, you will learn how to create your own amazing apps using App Inventor! You will find out how to connect up your computer to an Android phone or emulator. Then you'll discover how to build simple tools, games, and even how to code apps that use a camera. Keep on reading and you'll be on your way to becoming an expert app builder!

You will need both of these to create apps:

A computer to use the App Inventor website. (This can be a Mac or a PC.)

A Google account to log in and save your apps.

You will need one of the following to test your apps:

An Android device (this can be a phone or a tablet) and a special Android app called the **AI Companion.**

Some special software called an **Android emulator**. This will create a 'virtual Android Device' on your computer that you can use to test your apps.

The first few pages of this book will introduce you to App Inventor and explain how to add the basic components and code to an app. As you progress through the book, you will be using these techniques to build more powerful apps. Make sure you experiment, try out your own ideas and have fun!

CODE CAREFULLY AND AVOID THE BUGS!

Bugs are errors or mistakes in your code that stop your app working properly. Looking for these errors is called debugging. Make sure you enter your code really carefully. If things aren't working properly, see the tips on page 31 to help you.

GETTING STARTED

On this page, we will look at how to get your computer or device ready to create apps. Let's start with how to set up your computer.

Ask permission from an adult before entering the information to create an account.

STEP 1 – CREATE A GOOGLE ACCOUNT

So you can log in to App Inventor and save apps, you need to create a Google account.

⇨ Search for **create google account**.

create google account   **Search**

STEP 2 – SIGN IN

⇨ Sign in to your Google account.

Sign in

STEP 3 – VISIT THE APP INVENTOR WEBSITE

⇨ Type **appinventor.mit.edu** into your browser.

⇨ Click **Create apps!**

appinventor.mit.edu

Create apps!

IF YOU HAVE AN ANDROID DEVICE, FOLLOW THESE STEPS TO CONNECT IT TO APP INVENTOR

STEP 1 – DOWNLOAD THE COMPANION APP

⇨ Search for **app inventor companion app** on your Android device.

app inventor companion app   **Search**

⇨ Tap **Install** and follow the instructions.

https://accounts.google.com/signup?hl=en

MIT AI2 Companion
INSTALL

STEP 2 – CONNECT APP INVENTOR

⇨ Go back to your computer and make sure you are on the App Inventor site. Click **Create apps!**

Connect ▾
AI Companion
Emulator

⇨ Click the **Connect** menu, then choose **AI Companion**.

⇨ A QR code like this will appear on your computer.

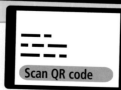

Scan QR code

⇨ Tap the **Scan QR code** button and hold your device camera up to the QR code on the computer screen.

STEPS IF YOU DON'T HAVE AN ANDROID DEVICE

STEP 1 – DOWNLOAD THE EMULATOR

⇨ Search for **download app inventor emulator**.

⇨ Choose **Mac** or **PC**, then follow the instructions to download the emulator.

STEP 2 – INSTALL THE EMULATOR

⇨ Some web browsers will then ask you to run the installation program. Choose **Run**.

⇨ If this does not happen, don't panic. The installer file should have been downloaded to your computer. Look in your **Downloads** folder for it. Double-click it to start installing the emulator. You should get a big grey box giving you instructions on what to do next. Follow these instructions to complete the installation.

⇨ If you are on a Mac when you try to install the emulator, you may get a security message. To install the app you will need to click **System Preferences**, click **Security** and change your settings to allow apps to run from **Anywhere**. Search for **install from unknown developer Mac** for more help.

≡ Recently Added:
    AI Starter

MIT App Inventor Tools >   AI Starter

STEP 3 – PC ONLY

If you are using a Mac you don't need to do this part.

⇨ On a PC, App Inventor needs a special program called the AI Starter to help it start the emulator. After you have installed the emulator it should run the AI Starter. The next time you use it, go to the Windows **Start** menu. It will be in the **MIT App Inventor** group or in the **Recently Added** section.

appinventor.mit.edu

Android Emulator

STEP 4 – CONNECT APP INVENTOR TO THE EMULATOR

⇨ To connect the App Inventor to the emulator, go back to the App Inventor website. Arrange your screen so the browser fills only part of the screen. Click **Create apps**.

Connect ▾
AI Companion
Emulator

Connecting
Companion starting...
[Cancel]

⇨ Click the **Connect** menu, then choose **Emulator**.

⇨ You should see a message telling you to wait while the emulator starts. Be patient – this may take a minute or two. App Inventor may ask you to select a project at this point. If so, move on to page 6 and start a project.

⇨ When the emulator has finished setting up, the app you are about to build will be shown on screen.

If App Inventor doesn't connect up to your device after following the steps on page 4, try closing the web browser on your computer. On your device, tap the **recent apps** button, then find the **MIT AI2 Companion App** icon and flick it upwards to close it. Restart the Companion App and restart the computer browser. Follow step 2 – Connect App Inventor on page 4 to reconnect.

If App Inventor doesn't connect up to your emulator, try closing the emulator, closing the web browser and starting again from step 3 above. If you still have problems connecting, go to the App Inventor site, click **Resources** then **Troubleshooting**.

⟩ SAYING HELLO

The first thing many computer programmers do when they try some new coding software is learn to make the software say 'Hello'. With our first app, we are going to make a program that says 'Hello world!'

STEP I – VISIT THE APP INVENTOR WEBSITE ▷

⇨ Open your web browser and visit **appinventor.mit.edu**

Create apps!

⇨ Click **Create apps!**

STEP 2 – SIGN IN ▷

⇨ Sign in to your Google account.

STEP 3 – START A NEW PROJECT ▷

⇨ At the top-left of the screen, click the **Start new project** button.

Start new project

⇨ Type in **hello** as the name for your project.

⇨ Click **OK**.

STEP 4 – DESIGN YOUR APP ▷

⇨ Add the objects or components you need for your app. Drag in a **Button** from the **User interface** group in the **Palette**.

⇨ Add a **Label** below it.

STEP 5 – SET PROPERTIES ▷

⇨ Change the text shown on the button and label.

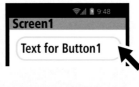

⇨ Click to select **Button1**.

⇨ The **Properties** box is on the right side of the screen. Near the bottom, find the **Text** property. Change it to say **Tap me**.

⇨ Click to select **Label1**.

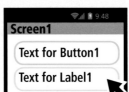

⇨ Find the **Text** property for the label. Change it to say **I'm waiting**.

STEP 6 – SWITCH TO THE BLOCKS VIEW ▷

⇨ We've used the **Designer** view to choose what the app looks like. Now we need to make our components work. At the the top-right of the screen, click the **Blocks** button.

STEP 7 – START CODING

We need to add code to make the button display 'Hello world!' when it is clicked or tapped.

⇨ First of all click the **Button1** icon.

⇨ Code blocks for the **Button1** component will appear.

⇨ Drag the **when Button1.Click** code block to the **Viewer**.

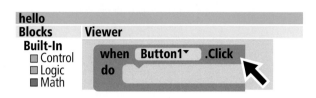

STEP 8 – SET THE TEXT

Screen1
Button1
☐ **Label1**

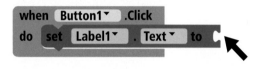

⇨ Click the **Label1** icon.

⇨ Scroll down to find the **set Label1.Text to** code block.

⇨ Drag it into the **when Button1. Click** code block.

STEP 9 – SAY HELLO

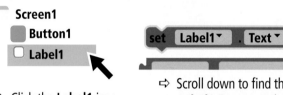

■ Math
■ **Text**
■ Lists

⇨ Click the **Text** group.

⇨ Find the code block at the top with a pair of empty quotation marks.

⇨ Drag it on to the end of the **set Label1.Text to** code block.

⇨ Type **Hello world!** between the quotes.

STEP 10 – TEST YOUR FIRST APP!

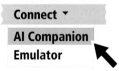

Connect ▾
AI Companion
Emulator

⇨ Click the **Connect** menu, then choose the **AI Companion** if you are using an Android device, or **Emulator** if you have installed it (see pages 4–5).

If you are using the emulator on a PC, make sure you have AI Starter running. (On a Mac it should start itself anyway.)

Or

If you are using an Android device, start the MIT AI Companion App, then connect it to your computer by using the QR Code option.

CUSTOMISE

• Change the message displayed when you tap the button.

• Experiment with the properties of the button and the label. Can you change their colour and size?

〈7〉

〉 TRANSLATOR

Our next project is going to be an interactive translator app. It will have a number of buttons that you can click to make the device speak a word or phrase in French. We will use a special component in AppInventor called **TextToSpeech** to make this work.

STEP 1 – PLANNING

Many developers draw diagrams and pictures to help them plan their apps.

Button components show words.

Pictures show other words or phrases.

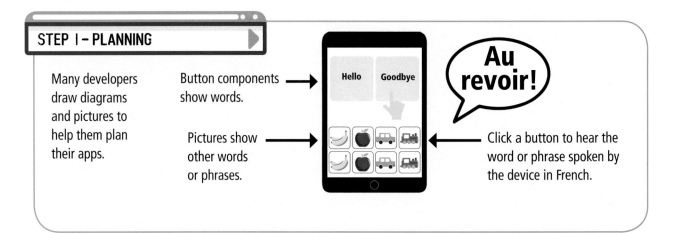

Click a button to hear the word or phrase spoken by the device in French.

STEP 2 – START A NEW PROJECT

⇨ Go to the App Inventor website. Click **Create Apps** and type in **translator** as a project name (see page 6).

STEP 3 – START DESIGNING

⇨ We need a row of buttons. To keep these lined up neatly we will use a **Layout** component, called **Horizontal Arrangement**. This acts like a box for us to put the buttons in.

⬜ **WebViewer**

Layout

⇨ Choose the **Layout** group from the bottom of the **Palette**.

⇨ We need the first component. Drag it onto the screen.

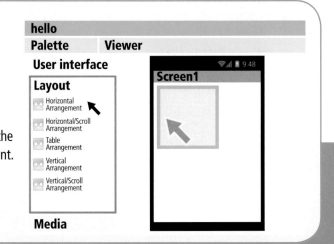

STEP 4 – ADD BUTTONS

➪ Drag a **Button** from the **User interface** group into the box on the screen.

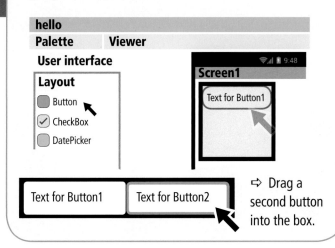

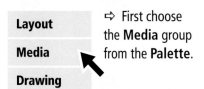

➪ Drag a second button into the box.

STEP 5 – SET PROPERTIES

➪ Change the text shown on the buttons.

➪ Click to select the first button.

➪ Go to **Properties** and find **Text**. Change the text to read **Hello**.

➪ Change the second button to read **Goodbye**.

STEP 6 – TEXT TO SPEECH

To enable our app to talk, we need to add a **TextToSpeech** component. It is a 'non-visible' component. This means we won't see it, but we will hear it!

➪ First choose the **Media** group from the **Palette**.

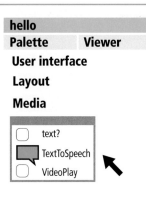

➪ Find the **TextToSpeech** component.

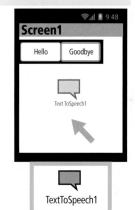

➪ Drag it onto the middle of the screen. It will be shown below the device.

STEP 7 – SWITCH VIEW

➪ Now we need to switch to the **Blocks** view. We can then add code that will make the buttons work.

Designer	Blocks

STEP 8 – START CODING

➪ Click on the **Button1** icon in the **Blocks** pane (see page 7).

➪ Code blocks for the **Button1** component will appear.

➪ Drag the **when Button1.Click** code block to the **Viewer**.

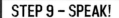

STEP 9 – SPEAK!

⇨ Click the **TextToSpeech1** icon.

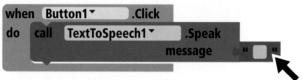

⇨ Find the **call TextToSpeech1.Speak message** code block.

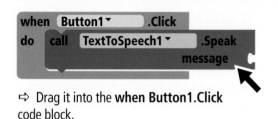

⇨ Drag it into the **when Button1.Click** code block.

STEP 10 – BONJOUR!

⇨ Click the **Text** group.

⇨ Find the code block at the top with a pair of empty quotation marks.

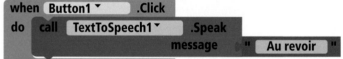

⇨ Drag it on to the end of the **call TextToSpeech1.Speak message** code block.

⇨ Type **Bonjour** between the quotes.

STEP 11 – AU REVOIR!

Our code means: When button1 is clicked, say 'Bonjour'.

⇨ Repeat steps 9 to 10 for the other button so it says **Au revoir**.

STEP 12 – TEST YOUR APP

⇨ Connect to the AI Companion app or the emulator (see pages 4–5) and test your app.

You should hear your device or emulator speak!

STEP 13 – IMPROVE YOUR ACCENT

⇨ We need to tell the app to speak with a French accent. This must happen before it does anything else. We will add a block of code that sets its accent as soon as the app initialises (starts).

⇨ Click the **Screen1** icon in the **Blocks** pane.

⇨ Code blocks for **Screen1** will appear.

⇨ Drag the **when Screen1.Initialize** code block to the **Viewer**.

⇨ Get this green code block from the **TextToSpeech1** icon.

⇨ Try testing your app again to see if it sounds different. You may need to force it to start again to get this new code block to run. You can do this by swapping around the position of the **Hello** and **Goodbye** buttons.

⇨ Get this pink code block from the **Text** group. Each language has its own code – FRA means France.

STEP 14 – PICTURES

Our app will look better and be easier to use if we add pictures. Start by searching online and downloading some suitable images, then upload them to App Inventor.

⇨ Open another tab in your browser. Search for an image you need.

⇨ Right-click one image.

XXCXZC X XZC
Save Image As...
XXCXZC X XZC

⇨ Click **Save Image As...**

 **Documents**

⇨ Navigate to your **Documents** folder then click **Save**.

Media

Upload File...

⇨ Click **Upload File...** (bottom-right of the screen).

Upload File...

Choose File... train.jpeg

Cancel   **OK**

⇨ Click **Choose File...** Browse for the image you downloaded. Finally click **OK**.

Media

train.jpeg

Upload File...

⇨ Your image should now be listed in the **Media** pane.

STEP 15 – PICTURE BUTTONS

You can use the image you uploaded to make a new button.

⇨ Add a new button (repeat step 4). Make sure it is selected.

⇨ Find the **Text** property (see step 5) and delete all the text.

⇨ Click the **Image** box.

⇨ Choose your new image and click **OK**. Your button will now have a picture on it.

Image

None
train.jpeg

Upload File...

Cancel   **OK**

⇨ Repeat steps 8 to 11 to make your new picture button speak. You could ask: 'Où est la gare?'

CUSTOMISE

• Add more buttons to the app for different words and phrases.

• Experiment with the properties of the buttons. Change their colour and size.

• Try creating an app for another language.

COUNTDOWN TIMER

A countdown app is a very useful thing to have on your phone or tablet. Once started it will count down from 30 seconds, showing the time left in large text. We will use a new component called the **Clock** to make some code run every second, and a **variable** called **t** to store the amount of time left.

STEP 1 – PLANNING

When the **Start** button is clicked the clock will start running.

 Every time the clock ticks it will make the variable **t** go down. ➡️ **t=8**

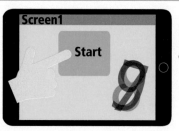

The amount of time left will be shown in this big label.

When the time left gets to zero, a sound effect will be played.

STEP 2 – START A NEW PROJECT

⇨ Add the objects or components you need for your app. Drag in a **Button** from the **User interface** group in the **Palette**.

⇨ Add a **Label** below it.

STEP 3 – DESIGN BASICS

⇨ Click to select the **Button** and change its text properties to say **Start**.

⇨ Select the **Label** and change its text properties to say **10** (see step 5, page 9).

Screen1

Start

10

STEP 4 – SET PROPERTIES

Button1

■ Default	
☐ Light Gray	**FontSize**
☐ Green	**20**
☐ Light Gray	

 ⇨ Change the **FontSize** to 20.

⇨ Set the background colour to **Green**.

Label1

⇨ Change the **FontSize** to 144.

Width

- ○ Automatic
- ○ Fill parent
- ○ ☐ pixels
- ● 100 percent

[Cancel] [OK]

⇨ Click the box below **Width**, then change it to be **100** per cent (the full width of the app).

TextAlignment

[left:0 ▾]

| left:0 |
| center:1 |
| right:2 |

⇨ Change the **TextAlignment** to centre it.

⇨ The screen is also a component that has properties. Select **Screen1**.

BackgroundColor

☐ White

☐ Orange

⇨ Set its background colour to **Orange**, or whichever colour you choose!

STEP 5 – ADD A CLOCK

We need a clock component to make the time go down every second. It is a 'non-visible' component.

➪ Choose the **Sensors** group from the **Palette**.

➪ Find the **Clock** component and drag it onto the middle of the screen. It will be shown below the device.

Clock1

STEP 6 – SOUND FILE

We need a sound effect to play when the time is up. You may already have some on your computer. If not, search online for a sound file to download and use.

➪ Open another tab in your browser. Search for a sound effect.

➪ Every website will be different. Find one that will let you download mp3 files.

Now upload your mp3 sound file to App Inventor.

➪ Click **Upload File...** (bottom-right of the screen).

| Upload File.. |
| Choose File... alarm.mp3 |
| Cancel   OK |

➪ Click **Choose File...** Browse for the sound you downloaded. It will probably be in your **Downloads** folder. Finally click **OK**.

Media

alarm.mp3

Upload File...

➪ Your sound file should now be listed in the **Media** pane.

STEP 7 – SOUND PLAYER

We need a **Sound** component to play the sound file. It is a 'non-visible' component.

➪ Choose the **Media** group from the **Palette**.

➪ Find the **Sound** component and drag it onto the middle of the screen. It will be shown below the device.

Clock1   Sound1

STEP 8 – PLAYER PROPERTIES

Now you need to set the sound player's properties so it plays the file you just uploaded.

➪ Click the **Source** box.

➪ Choose your new sound file and click **OK**. This will load your sound file into the **Player1** component.

None

alarm.mp3

Upload File...

Cancel   OK

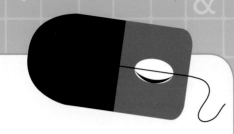

⇨ Now switch to the **Blocks** view and drag in these code blocks from the different groups. (See below for help.)

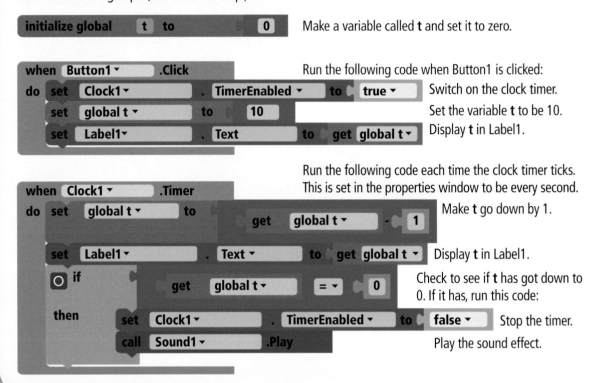

initialize global **t** to 0 — Make a variable called **t** and set it to zero.

when Button1 .Click — Run the following code when Button1 is clicked:
do set Clock1 . TimerEnabled to true — Switch on the clock timer.
set global t to 10 — Set the variable **t** to be 10.
set Label1 . Text to get global t — Display **t** in Label1.

Run the following code each time the clock timer ticks. This is set in the properties window to be every second.

when Clock1 .Timer
do set global t to get global t - 1 — Make **t** go down by 1.
set Label1 . Text to get global t — Display **t** in Label1.
if get global t = 0 — Check to see if **t** has got down to 0. If it has, run this code:
then set Clock1 . TimerEnabled to false — Stop the timer.
call Sound1 .Play — Play the sound effect.

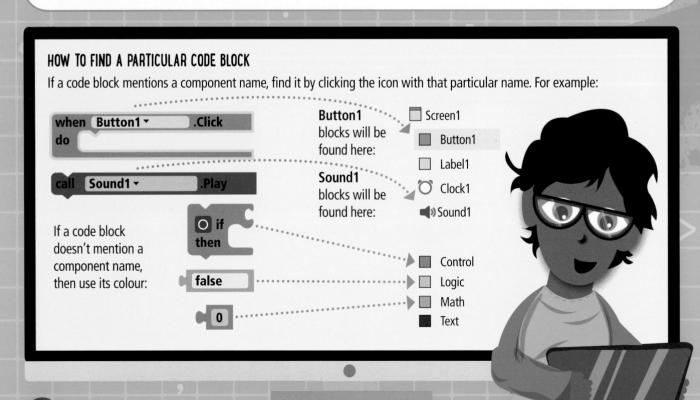

HOW TO FIND A PARTICULAR CODE BLOCK

If a code block mentions a component name, find it by clicking the icon with that particular name. For example:

when Button1 .Click
do

Button1 blocks will be found here:

call Sound1 .Play

Sound1 blocks will be found here:

☐ Screen1
☐ Button1
☐ Label1
○ Clock1
◀) Sound1

If a code block doesn't mention a component name, then use its colour:

if
then

false

0

▶ ☐ Control
▶ ☐ Logic
▶ ☐ Math
▶ ■ Text

Connect ▾
AI Companion
Emulator

⇨ Connect the AI Companion or the emulator.

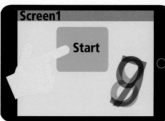

Screen1

Start

Test your app. Press the Start button and the app should count down 10 ... 9 ... 8 ... to 0, then play the sound effect.

⇨ If nothing happens, check all your code carefully and try again. See page 31 for more tips on debugging your code.

CUSTOMISE

• Change the length of the countdown from 10 to 30 seconds or more.

• Experiment with the properties of the components. Change their colour and size.

• Try using a different sound effect.

◀ **KEY CONCEPT**

VARIABLES

Variables are particular parts of a program that store data or information. They are different from ordinary numbers or strings because they can vary as a program runs. Each variable has a name, which is used to point to a part of the computer's memory. A value is then stored in that part of the memory.

A global variable is one that can be used by all the different parts of a program.

CLOCK (ALSO CALLED A TIMER)

When you want some code to run after a certain amount of time, or at regular intervals, use a clock component.

COMBINING BLOCKS

Sometimes code blocks need to be combined within others. This can be fiddly at first.
For example, the **if** code block below is built up block by block:

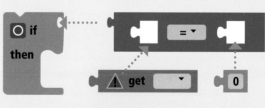

Remember, you may not find the exact block you see in the code listed in this book – sometimes you will have to use the drop-down menu to set the correct value or property.

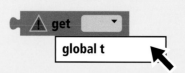

❯ PAINTING APP

This project is a simple painting app. Users can draw a picture by moving their finger across the screen. Buttons allow them to change colour or clear the screen. To make this app work, we will use a new component called the **Canvas**, which allows the app to paint using pixels, lines and circles.

STEP 1 – PLANNING

Tapping the new button will clear the **Canvas**.

The **Canvas** component takes up most of the screen.

The lines need to be about 10 pixels thick. We can set this when the app starts up.

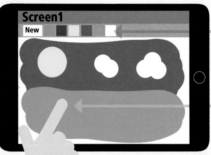

Add buttons for different colours. Clicking a button will set the drawing colour for the **Canvas**.

Tapping or clicking the **Canvas** will draw a circle at the current position of your finger.

Moving your finger (dragging it across the screen) will draw a line.

Just drawing straight lines will look a bit spikey.

Adding extra circles after each drag will make the line much smoother.

STEP 2 – START A NEW PROJECT

⇨ Go to the App Inventor website. Click **Create apps!** and use **painting** as a project name (see page 6).

⇨ Drag a **Horizontal Arrangement** component to the screen (see page 8).

⇨ Drag three buttons into the **Horizontal Arrangement** component (see page 9).

STEP 3 – ADD THE CANVAS

⇨ Choose the **Drawing and Animation** group from the **Palette**.

Drawing and Animation

⇨ Drag a **Canvas** component onto the screen below the buttons.

⇨ On the right-hand side of the screen in the **Properties** pane, change the properties for these components:

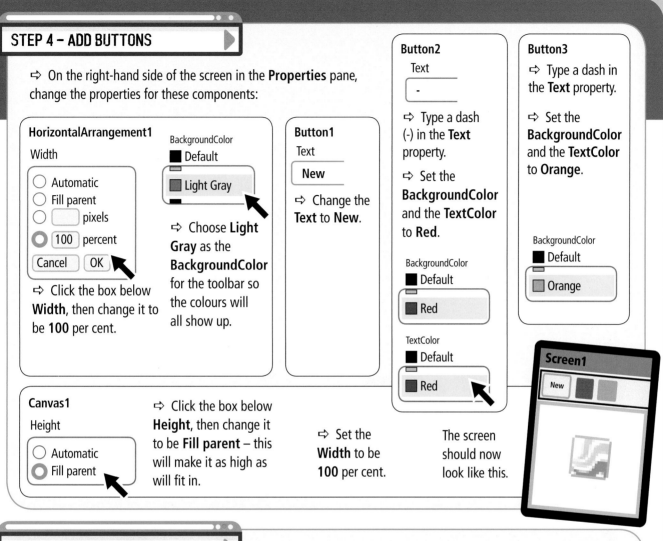

HorizontalArrangement1

Width

○ Automatic
○ Fill parent
○ ☐ pixels
◉ [100] percent
[Cancel] [OK]

⇨ Click the box below **Width**, then change it to be **100** per cent.

BackgroundColor
■ Default
☐ Light Gray

⇨ Choose **Light Gray** as the **BackgroundColor** for the toolbar so the colours will all show up.

Button1

Text
New

⇨ Change the **Text** to **New**.

Button2

Text
-

⇨ Type a dash (-) in the **Text** property.

⇨ Set the **BackgroundColor** and the **TextColor** to **Red**.

BackgroundColor
■ Default
■ Red

TextColor
■ Default
■ Red

Button3

⇨ Type a dash in the **Text** property.

⇨ Set the **BackgroundColor** and the **TextColor** to **Orange**.

BackgroundColor
■ Default
☐ Orange

Canvas1

Height

○ Automatic
◉ Fill parent

⇨ Click the box below **Height**, then change it to be **Fill parent** – this will make it as high as will fit in.

⇨ Set the **Width** to be **100** per cent.

The screen should now look like this.

Screen1
New ■ ■

⇨ Switch to the **Blocks** view, and drag in the code blocks below. To get the mustard coloured blocks, click each component's icon and pick from the menu in the **Viewer** pane. Get the green and purple blocks by clicking the **Canvas1** component.

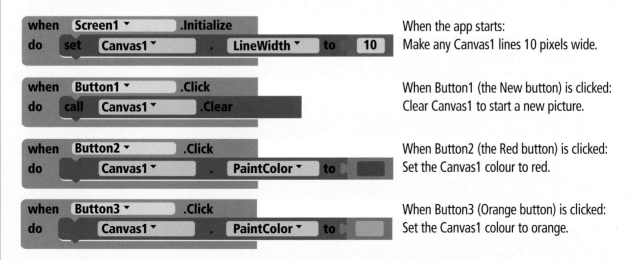

```
when  Screen1 ▾  .Initialize
do   set  Canvas1 ▾  .  LineWidth ▾  to  10
```
When the app starts:
Make any Canvas1 lines 10 pixels wide.

```
when  Button1 ▾  .Click
do   call  Canvas1 ▾  .Clear
```
When Button1 (the New button) is clicked:
Clear Canvas1 to start a new picture.

```
when  Button2 ▾  .Click
do   Canvas1 ▾  .  PaintColor ▾  to  ▢
```
When Button2 (the Red button) is clicked:
Set the Canvas1 colour to red.

```
when  Button3 ▾  .Click
do   Canvas1 ▾  .  PaintColor ▾  to  ▢
```
When Button3 (Orange button) is clicked:
Set the Canvas1 colour to orange.

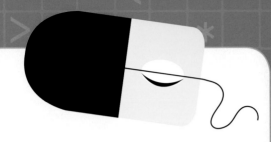

STEP 6 – TOUCH DOWN

⇨ This next part of the code will draw a circle on the **Canvas** when it is touched or clicked. Drag it onto the **Viewer**.

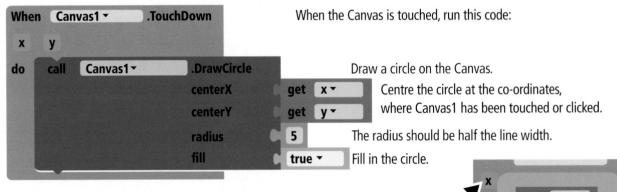

When the Canvas is touched, run this code:

Draw a circle on the Canvas.

Centre the circle at the co-ordinates, where Canvas1 has been touched or clicked.

The radius should be half the line width.

Fill in the circle.

⇨ To find the **get x** and **get y** code blocks, hover your mouse over the pink **x** box.

STEP 7 – TEST YOUR APP

⇨ Connect to the AI Companion or the emulator.

⇨ Test your app. Tap the screen and you should see a black dot appear. Test the colour buttons and try tapping the screen again.

STEP 8 – DRAW A LINE

⇨ This next part of the code will draw lines as you paint your picture. Drag it onto the **Viewer**.

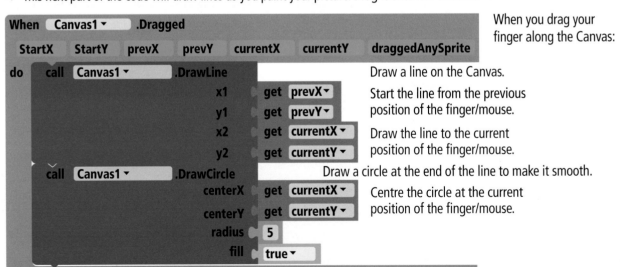

When you drag your finger along the Canvas:

Draw a line on the Canvas.

Start the line from the previous position of the finger/mouse.

Draw the line to the current position of the finger/mouse.

Draw a circle at the end of the line to make it smooth.

Centre the circle at the current position of the finger/mouse.

⇨ To find the get **prevX** and get **prevY** code blocks, hover your mouse over the pink **prevX** and **prevY** boxes.

STEP 9 – TEST AGAIN

⇨ Try drawing again on the app. You should now be able to make lines by moving your finger around.

 Try and draw something with your new app!

STEP 10 – MORE COLOUR

⇨ Add another button. Change its properties the way you did in step 4 and give it another colour.

⇨ Repeat parts of Step 5, adding code to make **Button4** set a new paint colour for **Canvas1**.

```
when  Button4 ▾  .Click
do  set  Canvas1  PaintColor ▾  to
```

CUSTOMISE

• Try making the line thicker. You will also need to change the radius of the circle that is drawn.

• Work out how to make a rubber – what would it need to do?

KEY CONCEPT

TOUCH START

When the user taps the device, this is called a touch event. It is used to trigger some code to run. The co-ordinates of where the user has touched the screen can be used by the code.

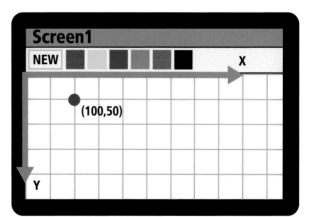

Co-ordinates

The **Canvas** events and drawing commands use **x** and **y** co-ordinates. The co-ordinates of the red point in the diagram above are x:100 and y:50.

The co-ordinates (0,0) will always be in the top left of the screen. The values that **x** and **y** go up to will depend on the size of the device.

> TAP THE BALL

In this simple game, the player has to catch a ball by tapping it as it bounces across the screen. The ball is a special type of image called an **ImageSprite**. This means it can be made to move around the **Canvas** easily. Two variables are used, one to keep track of the time and one as the score. The object of the game is to catch the ball as many times as possible in 30 seconds.

STEP 1 – PLANNING ▶

The score is stored in a variable and shown in this label.

score= 25

Tapping the ball will increase the score by 5 points. It will also make the ball jump to a new place and play a sound effect.

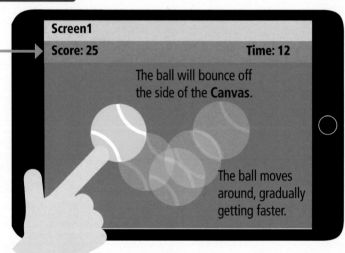

Screen1

Score: 25   **Time: 12**

The ball will bounce off the side of the **Canvas**.

The ball moves around, gradually getting faster.

Every time the clock ticks it will make the time variable go down.

↓

time = 12

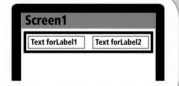

Game Over
Play again?

| Yes | No |

↑

When the time is up, this will be shown.

STEP 2 – START A NEW PROJECT ▶

⇨ Go to the App Inventor website. Click **Create apps!** and use **game1** as a project name.

⇨ Drag a **Horizontal Arrangement** component to the screen.

⇨ Drag two labels into the **Horizontal Arrangement** component.

Screen1

| Text forLabel1 | Text forLabel2 |

STEP 3 – ADD THE CANVAS ▶

⇨ Choose the **Drawing and Animation** group from the **Palette**.

⇨ Drag a **Canvas** component below the labels.

STEP 4 – ADD AN IMAGESPRITE ▶

⇨ Drag an **ImageSprite** component from the **Drawing and Animation** group on top of the **Canvas** component.

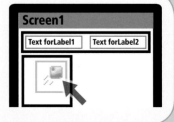

Screen1

| Text forLabel1 | Text forLabel2 |

STEP 5 – SET PROPERTIES ▶

⇨ On the right-hand side of the screen, in the properties window, change the properties for the following components:

HorizontalArrangement1

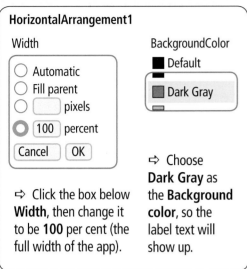

Width

- ○ Automatic
- ○ Fill parent
- ○ ☐ pixels
- ● 100 percent
- Cancel | OK

BackgroundColor

- ■ Default
- ▨ Dark Gray

⇨ Choose **Dark Gray** as the **Background color**, so the label text will show up.

⇨ Click the box below **Width**, then change it to be **100** per cent (the full width of the app).

Label1

Text

Score: 0

⇨ Add the **Text** property as **Score: 0**.

TextColor

- ■ Default
- ☐ Yellow

⇨ Set the **TextColor** to **Yellow**.

FontSize

20

⇨ Set the **FontSize** to **20**.

Label2

⇨ Add the **Text** property as **Time: 30**.

⇨ Set the **TextColour** to **Yellow**.

⇨ Set the **FontSize** to **20**.

Width

Fill parent

⇨ **Label2** must be over on the right-hand side, so set its **Width** to **Fill parent**.

TextAlignment

- left : 0 ▾
- left : 0
- right : 2

⇨ Finally set its **TextAlignment** to **right**.

Canvas1

Height

- ○ Automatic
- ● Fill parent

⇨ Click the box below **Height**, then change it to **Fill parent**. This will make it as high as will fit in the screen.

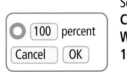

⇨ Set the **Canvas1 Width** to be **100** per cent.

STEP 6 – ADD AN IMAGE ▶

tennis ball

Search

⇨ To add an image to your game, open another tab in your browser. Search for the image you need.

Media

Upload File...

⇨ To upload your image to App Inventor, click **Upload File...** (bottom right of the screen).

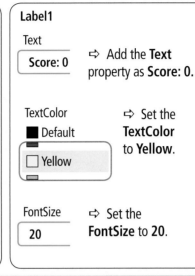

⇨ Right-click the image.

XXCXZC X XZC
Save Image As...
XXCXZC X XZC

⇨ Click **Save Image As...**

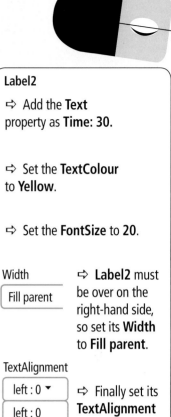

🗋 **Documents**

⇨ Navigate to your **Documents** folder then click **Save**.

Upload File..

Choose File...   ball.png

Cancel   OK

⇨ Click **Choose File...** Browse for the image you downloaded. Finally click **OK**.

⇨ Your image should now be listed in the **Media** pane.

STEP 7 – IMAGESPRITE PROPERTIES ▶

Picture

None
ball.png

Upload File...

Cancel   **OK**

⇨ Click the **ImageSprite** to select it.

⇨ Set its **Picture** property to the new uploaded file.

⇨ Set its **Width** and **Height** to be around **60** pixels.

⇨ Choose the **Interval** property. Try **25** to start with. The **Interval** property tells the app how often to move the **ImageSprite**.

STEP 8 – ADD NON-VISIBLE COMPONENTS ▶

⇨ The app needs a **Clock** component to make the time go down every second and a **Sound** component to play sound effects. It will also need an mp3 sound file. Follow page 13 steps 5, 6, 7 and 8 to get these components set up.

⇨ The app will need to show a message box when the game ends. To code this you will need to add a **Notifier** component.

Clock1 Sound1 Notifier1

STEP 9 – STARTUP CODE ▶

⇨ Switch to the **Blocks** view, and drag in these code blocks.

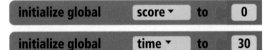

initialize global score ▾ to 0   Make a variable called **score** and set it to 0.

initialize global time ▾ to 30   Make a variable called **time** and set it to 30.

⇨ There are several things we need to reset each time a game starts. To avoid repeating all the code, we will create a new command called **startNewGame**. Programmers call this a function or procedure.

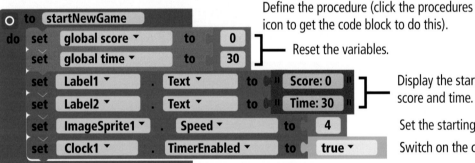

Define the procedure (click the procedures icon to get the code block to do this).

Reset the variables.

Display the starting score and time.

Set the starting speed for the ball.

Switch on the clock (timer).

⇨ We have now defined the procedure called **startNewGame** but not actually run any of the code yet! To do this we need to call the procedure:

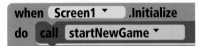

When the app starts:

Call the startNewGame procedure (this runs all the code we added in above).

⇨ Test your code so far on your device or the emulator. The ball should move across the screen and stop when it hits the edge.

STEP 10 – BOUNCE CODE ▶

⇨ Add the following code blocks to make the ball bounce.

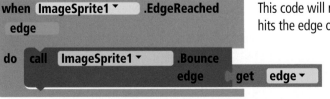

This code will run when the ball hits the edge of the screen.

Make the ball bounce. (Hover over the pink **edge** box to find the **get edge** block.)

STEP 11 - TAP CODE

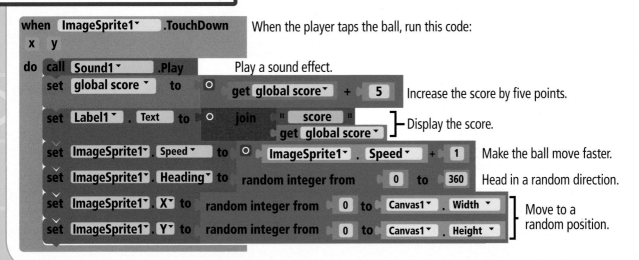

```
when  ImageSprite1▾  .TouchDown
  x  y
```
When the player taps the ball, run this code:

```
do  call  Sound1▾  .Play
```
Play a sound effect.

```
set  global score▾  to  ○  get global score▾  +  5
```
Increase the score by five points.

```
set  Label1▾ . Text  to  ○  join  "  score  "
                               get global score▾
```
Display the score.

```
set  ImageSprite1▾ . Speed▾  to  ○  ImageSprite1▾ . Speed▾  +  1
```
Make the ball move faster.

```
set  ImageSprite1▾ . Heading▾  to  random integer from  0  to  360
```
Head in a random direction.

```
set  ImageSprite1▾ . X▾  to  random integer from  0  to  Canvas1▾ . Width▾
set  ImageSprite1▾ . Y▾  to  random integer from  0  to  Canvas1▾ . Height▾
```
Move to a random position.

STEP 12 - CLOCK CODE

⇨ For each second that passes, the time variable needs to go down by one. When it gets to zero, the app needs to display the **Play again?** message.

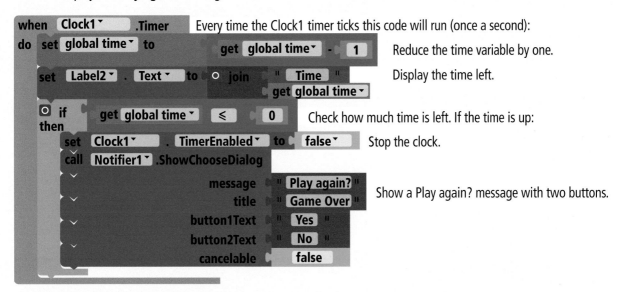

```
when  Clock1▾  .Timer
```
Every time the Clock1 timer ticks this code will run (once a second):

```
do  set global time▾  to  get global time▾  -  1
```
Reduce the time variable by one.

```
set  Label2▾ . Text▾  to  ○  join  "  Time  "
                               get global time▾
```
Display the time left.

```
if  get global time▾  ≤  0
then
```
Check how much time is left. If the time is up:

```
set  Clock1▾ . TimerEnabled▾  to  false▾
```
Stop the clock.

```
call  Notifier1▾ .ShowChooseDialog
              message  "  Play again?  "
                title  "  Game Over  "
          button1Text  "  Yes  "
          button2Text  "  No  "
          cancelable  false
```
Show a Play again? message with two buttons.

⇨ If the player clicks **Yes**, then we need to run the **startNewGame** procedure, or else the app needs to close.

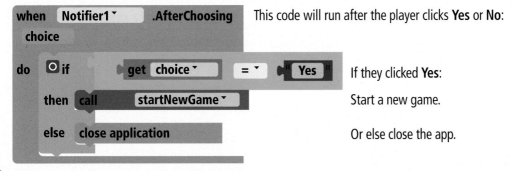

```
when  Notifier1▾  .AfterChoosing
  choice
```
This code will run after the player clicks **Yes** or **No**:

```
do  if  get choice▾  =▾  "  Yes  "
```
If they clicked **Yes**:

```
then  call  startNewGame▾
```
Start a new game.

```
else  close application
```
Or else close the app.

› PHOTO PAINTER

This app will let you take a photo using the camera on your tablet or phone. (Depending on your computer, you may not be able to run this on the emulator.) The photo will be shown on a **Canvas**. Using the ideas from the Painting App on page 16, you will be able to draw on the photo: add sunglasses, extra hair or anything else you want! Finally, a **Save** button will let you save your creations.

STEP 1 – PLANNING

Tap the **Snap** button to take a photo.

The **Camera** component will be needed.

storage/emulated/0/5624.png

The **Save** button will save a copy of the image.

Add buttons for different colours. Clicking one will set the current drawing colour.

Draw on the top of the photo.

STEP 2 – COMPONENTS

⇨ Go to the App Inventor website. Click **Create apps!** and use **photopic** as a project name.

⇨ You need a **HorizontalArrangement** component, **Buttons** and a **Canvas** component. Follow page 16 steps 2, 3 and 4 to get these components set up.

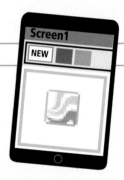

STEP 3 – SAVE BUTTON

⇨ Drag another **Button** in between the **New** and red button. Set its text to read **Save** and change the **New** button text to **Snap**.

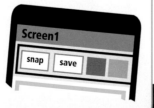

STEP 4 – ADD THE CAMERA

⇨ The app needs a **Camera** component to take the photo. You can find it in the **Media** group. Drag the **Camera** component to the middle of the screen. It should appear at the bottom.

camera1

STEP 5 – COLOUR CODING

⇨ Now switch to the **Blocks** view. Drag in **set Canvas1.LineWidth to** when the app starts up.

```
when   Screen1           .Initialize
do    set    Canvas1   .    LineWidth   to   10
```

⇨ Drag in this code to set the painting colour.

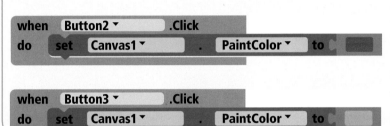

```
when   Button2    .Click
do    set    Canvas1   .    PaintColor   to  [    ]
```

When Button2 (the red button) is clicked: Set the Canvas paint colour to red.

```
when   Button3    .Click
do    set    Canvas1   .    PaintColor   to  [    ]
```

When Button3 (orange button) is clicked: Set the Canvas paint colour to orange.

STEP 6 – DRAWING CODE

⇨ You need to add the following code to make the **Canvas** draw a dot when you tap it with your finger.

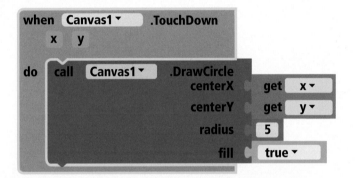

```
when   Canvas1    .TouchDown
       x   y
do   call   Canvas1   .DrawCircle
                        centerX   get   x
                        centerY   get   y
                        radius    5
                        fill      true
```

⇨ You need to add the code below to make the **Canvas** draw a line when you drag your finger across the screen.

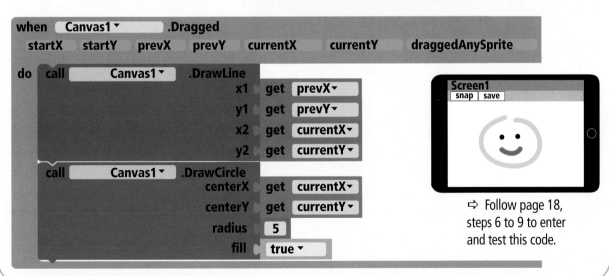

```
when   Canvas1    .Dragged
   startX   startY   prevX   prevY   currentX   currentY   draggedAnySprite
do   call       Canvas1   .DrawLine
                          x1   get   prevX
                          y1   get   prevY
                          x2   get   currentX
                          y2   get   currentY
      call       Canvas1   .DrawCircle
                          centerX   get   currentX
                          centerY   get   currentY
                          radius    5
                          fill      true
```

Screen1
snap save

⇨ Follow page 18, steps 6 to 9 to enter and test this code.

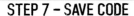

STEP 7 – SAVE CODE

⇨ Next, we need to enter some code to make the **Save** button work.
First of all we will make a variable that will store the name of the file.
Then we need to call the **Canvas SaveAs** command. Add the following code:

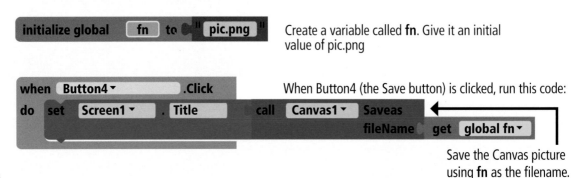

Create a variable called **fn**. Give it an initial value of pic.png

When Button4 (the Save button) is clicked, run this code:

Save the Canvas picture using **fn** as the filename.

STEP 8 – CAMERA

⇨ When the **Camera** button is clicked, we need the **call Camera1.TakePicture** command to take the picture. We also need to make sure that each time a new picture is taken it has a new filename. We can do this by generating a random name.

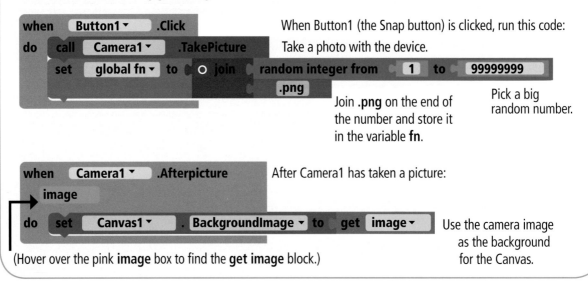

When Button1 (the Snap button) is clicked, run this code:
Take a photo with the device.

Pick a big random number.

Join **.png** on the end of the number and store it in the variable **fn**.

After Camera1 has taken a picture:

Use the camera image as the background for the Canvas.

(Hover over the pink **image** box to find the **get image** block.)

Test your code so far. Try taking a photo with the **Snap** button then drawing over it. Use the **Save** button to keep a copy of your picture. (To find the picture you have saved, click the **My Files** icon on your device home screen. It may not show up in your **Gallery** folder depending on how it is set up.)

STEP 9 – PICK A LINE

You can add an extra feature to allow people to draw with a thin, thick or medium line.

⇨ Click the **Designer** button. Find the **Spinner** component in the **User interface** group and drag it onto the screen.

Screen1

snap | save | | | Spinner

Properties

Spinner1

ElementsFromString

1,2,5,10,20

Width

50 pixels...

⇨ Now set the properties for the **Spinner**. The **ElementsFromString** property needs a range of values that people can choose from for the line thickness. Type in 1,2,5,10,20, or your own values, and separate each value with a comma, but no spaces.

⇨ Set the **Width** to **50** pixels.

STEP 10 – CODE THE LINE

⇨ To make the **Spinner** code work, you need to add these code blocks.

```
when    Spinner1 ▼  .AfterSelecting
    selection
do  set  Canvas1 ▼  . LineWidth ▼  to  get selection ▼
```

After the selection has been made with the Spinner:

Set the new line thickness. (Find the **get selection** block by hovering over the pink **selection** box.)

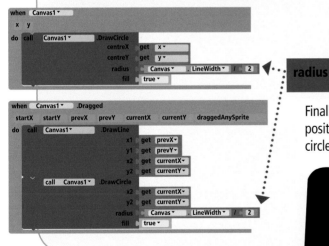

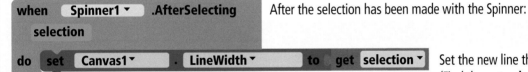

```
radius    Canvas1 ▼  . LineWidth ▼  /  2
```

Finally, change the radius of the circle drawn in the two positions shown on the left (from page 25, step 6). Make the circle approximately half the width of the new line thickness.

CUSTOMISE

• Add extra buttons to change colours, repeating step 2 and step 5.

• Allow users to choose their own file names, by adding a **Notifier** component and using a **ShowTextDialog** command.

› SHARING YOUR APPS

Once you have completed an app, you might want to share it with family or friends. You can do this in a number of ways. App Inventor will let you download the app so you can email it to people. You could share it via a QR code or by uploading it to an app store.

SHARING BY EMAIL

STEP 1 – CREATE AN APK FILE ▶

⇨ First of all, make sure you have completed your app and tested it.

⇨ App Inventor will then make a special file called an **APK** file and download it to your computer. **APK** stands for Android Application Package.

Build ▾ **Help** ▾

App (provide QR code for .apk)

App (save .apk to my computer)

📁 Desktop	📄 painting app.apk
📁 Documents	
⬛ Downloads	
📁 Photos	

⇨ Click **Build** and then **App (save .apk to my computer).**

⇨ Your APK file will be found in your **Downloads** folder.

STEP 2 – EMAIL THE APK FILE ▶

⇨ Start a new email in the usual way.

Compose Email:

To:

Cc:

Subject:

Attach: 📄 painting app.apk

Send

Type in the address of the person you are sending the app to.

Choose a subject for your email – maybe **Try my new App!**

Browse to find the APK file in your **Dowloads** and attach it to your email.

Type in your message.

Click **Send.**

STEP 3 - INSTALLING THE APK FILE

⇨ Once someone has been sent your app by email, they need to tap on the attached APK file to download it.

⇨ They will then need to tap it again to run the APK file.

⇨ Depending on how their device is set up, they may get a warning. This is beacuse downloading apps can be unsafe. Some apps may contain viruses that can delete files on your device, or stop it working properly. Other dangerous apps may even access your photos or information.

If they want to download your app, they will probably have to click the **Settings** button to allow the app to be downloaded.

painting app.apk

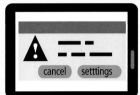

cancel setttings

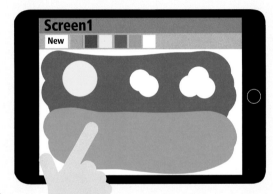

Screen1

New

An icon for the app should then be added to the home screen. Tapping on the icon should start up your app!

SHARING BY QR CODE

If you want to share your app with someone who can see your computer, you can just use a temporary QR code.

Build ▾ **Help ▾**

App (provide QR code for .apk)

App (save .apk to my computer)

⇨ Click **Build** and then **App (provide QR code for .apk)**.

⇨ App Inventor will create the APK file as in step 1. It will then show a QR code that contains a link to downloading your app.

⇨ Your friends and family can then use a QR reader to download the app.

⇨ Following step 3 above will install the app on their device.

SHARING THROUGH AN APP STORE

⇨ There are various app stores that allow you to buy, sell or share apps. To share an app you have created, start by downloading the APK file as in step 1. To upload this file to an app store, search online for more information about app stores and choose a suitable one. Remember to check with an adult before you use one.

GLOSSARY

ANDROID The name of the software used to run many phones and tablets.

BUG An error in a program that stops it working properly.

CANVAS A component that can be painted on with special drawing commands.

CODE BLOCK A draggable instruction icon used in App Inventor.

COMMAND A specific word that tells a computer to do something.

COMPONENT An object such as a button or label added to an app.

CO-ORDINATES The position of something, using **x** and **y** values to describe how far across and up it is from the centre of the component.

DEBUG To remove bugs (or errors) from a program.

DEVICE A smartphone or tablet.

EMULATOR A 'virtual smartphone or tablet' running on a computer, behaving the same way that a real device would.

EVENT Something that has happened while a program is running, such as a component being clicked or touched.

FUNCTION A reusable section of code combining a number of commands.

IMAGESPRITE An object with a picture on it that moves around.

INTEGER A whole number, such as 1, 2 or 3 (not a fraction).

PIXEL The size of one of the small dots on a computer screen, used as a measuring unit.

PROCEDURE Several commands that in combination do something.

QR CODE (QUICK REPSONSE CODE) A pattern of black and white squares that can be read by a special app on a smartphone, linking to a web address or some data.

RADIUS The distance from the centre to the edge of a circle.

RANDOM A number that can't be predicted.

RIGHT-CLICK Clicking the right mouse button on a sprite or icon.

STRING A series of characters (letters or symbols), often stored in a variable.

USER INTERFACE Components that allow the user to interact with a program.

VARIABLE A value used to store information in a program that can change.

CHECKLIST

The App Inventor website has lots of useful information, including a section on troubleshooting. For more help, go to the App Inventor website, click the **Resources** menu then choose **Troubleshooting**.

BUGS AND DEBUGGING

When you find your code isn't working as expected, stop and look though each piece of code you have put in. Here are some things to check:

TIPS TO REDUCE BUGS

⇨ If you are making your own app, spend time planning it before you start.

⇨ Practise debugging! Make a very simple app and get a friend to change some blocks of code while you're not looking. Can you fix it?

⇨ When things are working properly, spend time looking through your code so you understand each line. To be good at debugging, you need to understand what each line of your code does and how your code works.

Can't connect?

appinventor.mit.edu

MIT App Inventor 2

Scan QR code

If you can't connect App Inventor to your device or emulator try restarting them (see the bottom of page 4 and 5).

Not updating?

If you have changed code but it doesn't seem to be running, try moving around some of the components. This will force App Inventor to run all the code again. This can often be an issue when you have code in the **Screen1. Initialize** block – this will only get updated if the screen is 'rebuilt' after it changes.

when Screen1 ▾ .Initialize
do

Right component, wrong event?

when Canvas1 ▾ .TouchDown

when Canvas1 ▾ .TouchUp

They may look the same at first glance, but check you have the correct event blocks. For example, **when Canvas1. TouchUp** will make your code run at a different time to **when Canvas1.TouchDown!**

Wrong size or wrong shape?

Width

○ Automatic
○ Fill parent
○ ☐ pixels
● 100 percent
Cancel   OK

Check your properties carefully. For example, 100 per cent is not the same as 100 pixels. Have you set **Width** instead of **Height**?

No sound?

None
alarm.mp3

Upload File...
Cancel   OK

If you you have added a sound component and coded it to play when a button is clicked but there is still no sound, check you have also uploaded and set the sound file properties.

INDEX

Published in Great Britain in 2018 by Wayland

Text copyright © ICT Apps Ltd, 2017
Art and design copyright © Hodder and Stoughton Limited, 2017

Editor: Catherine Brereton
Freelance editor: Hayley Fairhead
Designer: Peter Clayman
Illustrator: Maria Cox

ISBN: 978 1 5263 0107 9
10 9 8 7 6 5 4 3 2 1

Wayland
An imprint of
Hachette Children's Group
Part of Hodder & Stoughton
Carmelite House
50 Victoria Embankment
London EC4Y 0DZ

An Hachette UK Company
www.hachette.co.uk
www.hachettechildrens.co.uk

Printed in China

The website addresses (URLs) included in this book were valid at the time of going to press. However, it is possible that contents or addresses may have changed since the publication of this book. No responsibility for any such changes can be accepted by either the author or the Publisher.

E-safety
Children will need access to the internet for most of the activities in this book. Parents or teachers should supervise this and discuss staying safe online with children.